My First Book of Questions

My First Book

Easy Answers to Hard

Copyright © 1992 by Grey Castle Press.
All rights reserved. Published by Scholastic Inc.

CARTWHEEL BOOKS is a trademark of Scholastic Inc.

LIBRARY OF CONGRESS CATALOGING-IN-PUBLICATION DATA

My first book of questions: easy answers to hard questions children
ask / illustrated by Lena Shiffman . . . [et al.].
    p.   cm. — (Cartwheel learning bookshelf)
    Summary: Includes sixty questions which are alphabetically
arranged and illustrated covering various topics such as nature,
technology, personal relations, and cultural customs.
  ISBN 0-590-44942-7
  1. Children's questions and answers. [1. Questions and answers.]
I. Shiffman, Lena. II. Title: My first book of questions.
III. Series.
AG195.M39 1992
031.02—dc20   91-40168
                                      CIP
                                      AC

12 11 10 9 8 7 6 5 4 3 2 1   2 3 4 5 6 7/9

Printed in Singapore
First Scholastic printing, September 1992

# of Questions

Questions Children Ask

Written by Jennifer Daniel, Ann Hodgman, and Ann Whitman

Illustrated by Robin Brickman, Marie DeJohn, George Ford, Pam Johnson, Laura Kelly, Mike McDermott, Anita Nelson, Carol Schwartz, Lena Shiffman, Joel Snyder, and Richard Walz

Cartwheel
·B·O·O·K·S· ™

SCHOLASTIC INC.

New York Toronto London Auckland Sydney

TABLE OF CONTENTS

A a

What is **AIR**?

We cannot see air, or taste it, or smell it, but air is all around us. Air is a mixture of clear gases that surrounds the earth.

Most of air is made up of a gas called *nitrogen*. Another part is made up of a gas called *oxygen*. A very small part is made up of *helium*. Helium is the gas put inside some balloons so that they can float by themselves!

We take air into our lungs each time we breathe. All plants and animals on earth need air in order to live and grow. That is why it is important to keep our air clean.

What makes an **AIRPLANE** fly?

An airplane has *engines* that make the power to move the plane. As the plane moves forward, it pushes the air out of its way, and the air has to move around it. The wings of an airplane are curved so that the air flows around them easily. This air pushes against the wings of the airplane and keeps it up in the sky.

Earth's gravity keeps pulling at the plane to come down. But the power of the engine keeps the plane up in the air. When the pilot wants the plane to go higher, he or she speeds up the engines. And when the pilot wants to land the plane, he or she slows down the engines so that the plane comes down slowly.

Bb

What's inside a **BASEBALL**?

A baseball is round and white, with evenly spaced stitches that hold the leather cover in place.

Just underneath the cover is a layer of fibers or threads. These threads are wound around a core. Professional baseballs have a central core of cork — a soft wood that comes from a certain kind of tree. Others may have a filler made of tightly packed scraps of newspaper or even plastic, molded into a tightly formed ball.

A baseball is firm enough to be hit very hard by a bat. The ball can travel a long way — all the way over the fence for a home run. But the fibers underneath the cover make the ball soft enough for you to catch it safely in your glove.

A softball is like a baseball, but softballs are larger and heavier, with a thicker layer of fibers.

When is my **BIRTHDAY**?

Your birthday is the anniversary of the day you were born. You celebrate it at the same time every year — the same month, the same date. And each year you are one year older. Because it comes only once a year, it can seem like forever until your birthday arrives.

There are twelve months in every year and about 30 days in every month. After your birthday party, where everyone wishes you "Happy Birthday!", you have to wait another 365 days (that's twelve months) until the next one.

FEBRUARY						
	1	2	3	4	5	6
7	8	9	10	11	12 Lincoln's Birthday	13
14	15	16	17	18	19	20
21	22 Washington's Birthday	23	24	25 My Birthday	26	27
28						

What is **BLOOD** and what does it do?

Blood is a liquid that flows through every part of your body. If you've ever gotten a cut or a nosebleed, you know what blood looks like. But you may not know how many important jobs blood does.

Blood carries air and food to your body's cells so that they can grow the way they should. It helps fight germs that might make you sick. And it helps clean wastes out of your body. Wastes are things your body doesn't need.

Your *heart* is the pump that keeps your blood moving. It pumps blood through tiny tubes called *arteries* and *veins*.

Your whole body needs blood. You can't get along without it! But don't worry if you do get a little cut or nosebleed. Your body is making more blood all the time.

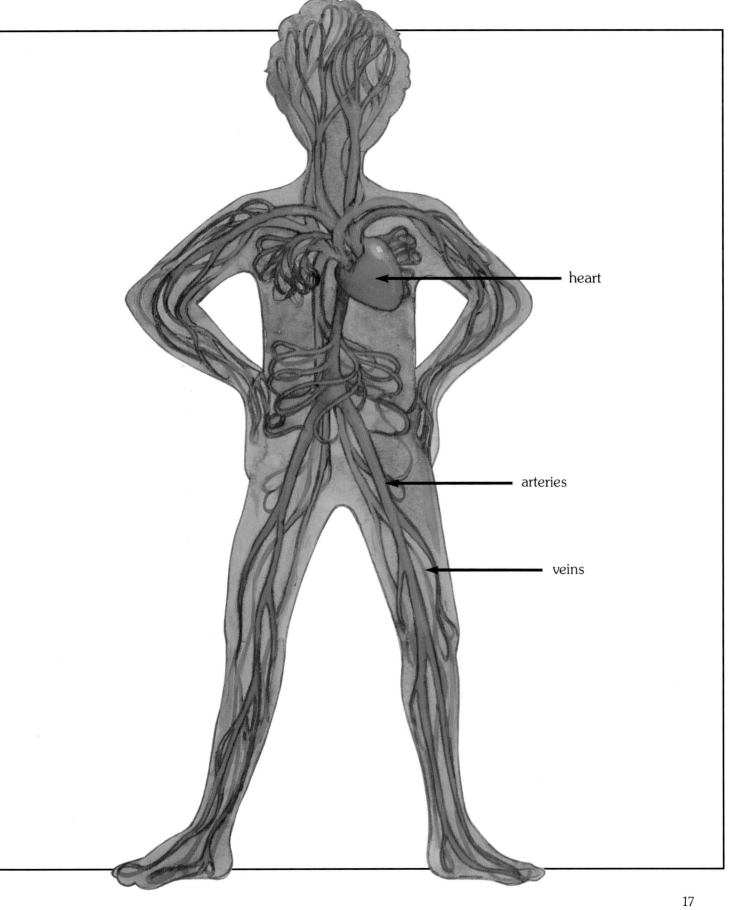

heart

arteries

veins

What is the tallest **BUILDING**?

The tallest building in the world is the *Sears Tower* in Chicago, Illinois. It took almost four years to build and was finished in 1973. The Sears Tower has 110 floors and rises to 1,454 feet! People work in offices there.

From the top of the Sears Tower on a clear day, you can see four states — Illinois, Michigan, Indiana, and Wisconsin. Sometimes when it's really windy, the building will sway back and forth just a little — no more than a few inches.

The outside of the Sears Tower is made of glass. When light hits the glass in a certain way, it reflects parts of the city and the sky. So the Sears Tower sometimes looks like a huge mirror.

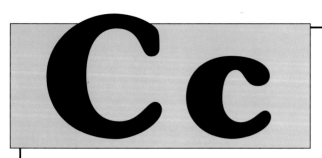

Why do **CAMELS** have humps?

Camels can travel for days and days across the hot desert without eating or drinking. They can do this because of their humps! The hump is where a camel stores its food and water. Before starting on a long trip, a camel eats and drinks so much that a huge hump of fat grows on its back. The camel can live on this stored-up food and water for many days.

The camel lives in the countries of North Africa and the Middle East where there are huge deserts. Because deserts are very hot, very dry, and full of sand, there are not many plants or other things to eat. Very few animals can live in the desert.

What makes a **CAR** go?

Energy is what makes a car go. Just as your body needs food to give you energy to run around the playground, a car needs gasoline to give it the energy to move.

Gasoline is stored in the tank. When it moves into the engine, the gasoline burns. The more gas that burns, the more energy there is to make the engine parts move. Because the engine is connected to the wheels, they are forced to move, too. When the wheels turn, the car goes!

gas tank

engine

Dd

What causes **DAY** and night?

Day and night are caused by the earth turning. As the earth moves through space, it slowly *rotates,* or spins. It takes 24 hours for the earth to spin completely around. During those 24 hours, we have one night and one day.

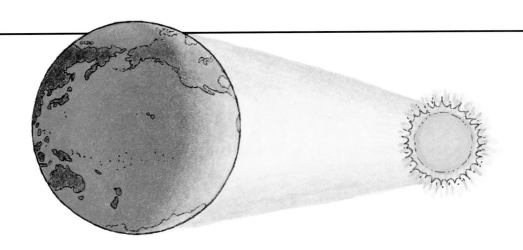

Since the earth is spinning, sometimes the part you are on faces the sun and sometimes it does not. Night is when the part of the earth that you are on faces away from the sun.

When you are getting up to go to school, someone on the other side of the earth is getting ready to go to bed!

What are **DINOSAURS**?

Dinosaurs are animals that lived millions of years ago, before there were any people. The name dinosaur means "terrible lizard." We know about the dinosaurs from the clues they left behind, like footprints and bones. These clues are called *fossils*.

Some dinosaurs had big fat bodies, long skinny necks, and tiny heads. Others had spikes all along their backs and tails. Still others were only about the size of a large house cat.

Most dinosaurs lived on land. But the gigantic *Brachiosaurus* spent most of its life in the water. This monster was taller than a three-story building! Another kind of dinosaur is the *Pteranodon*. It could glide through the air on wings that were 25-feet long.

What is **DIVORCE**?

Sometimes, when a husband and wife aren't happy living together, they decide to end their marriage. Then we say that they are getting a divorce. Although divorced moms and dads do not live in the same house anymore, they try to work out ways to share the care of their children.

After a divorce, sometimes one parent, or both of them, decides to marry someone else. A mother's new husband is called a stepfather by her children. A father's new wife is called a stepmother by his children. And if that stepfather or stepmother has children from a first marriage, these children are called stepbrothers and stepsisters.

What is a **DREAM** and what is a nightmare?

While you sleep, your mind is still working and thinking. A dream is made up of the ideas and feelings that are going on in your brain. Often some little thing you thought about during the day, like a peanut butter sandwich, will pop up in a dream. But dreams don't always seem to make much sense.

A nightmare is the kind of dream that makes you feel scared or upset. If you dream of a scary monster chasing you, that is a nightmare. But if that monster says, "Wait up! I just want to share my candy bar with you," that nightmare can turn into a sweet dream.

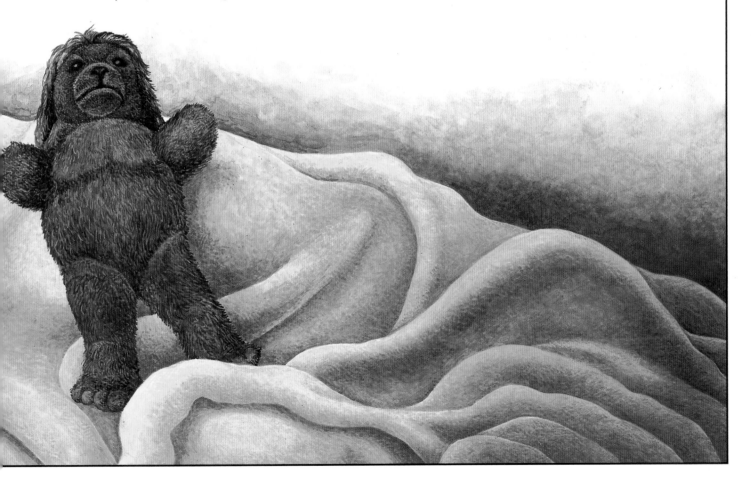

What's inside the **EARTH**?

If you could dig deep enough under the grass and soil you would come to a layer of rocks that goes down for about twenty miles. The dirt and the rocks below them make up the earth's *crust*. Some of these rocks were made by volcanoes. Others were carried there by glaciers, which were great sheets of ice that covered the earth millions of years ago.

Under the earth's crust is a very thick layer of hot rocks called the *mantle*. And under the mantle, at the center of the earth, is the *core*. The outer part of the core is believed to be liquid, while the inner part may be solid.

What is an **ECHO**?

Whenever you make a noise, you are making waves of sound that travel through the air. Although you can't see these sound waves, they touch things all around you. Usually, the sound waves fade as they travel. But sometimes the sound waves hit something and bounce back. Then you can hear the same sound twice. That's an echo. It's like a ball that bounces back toward you when you throw it against a wall.

Echoes are usually clearest and strongest if the sound waves bounce off a hard, smooth surface. If you clap your hands or shout "Hello!" in a tunnel, you may hear an echo as the sound waves bounce off the wall.

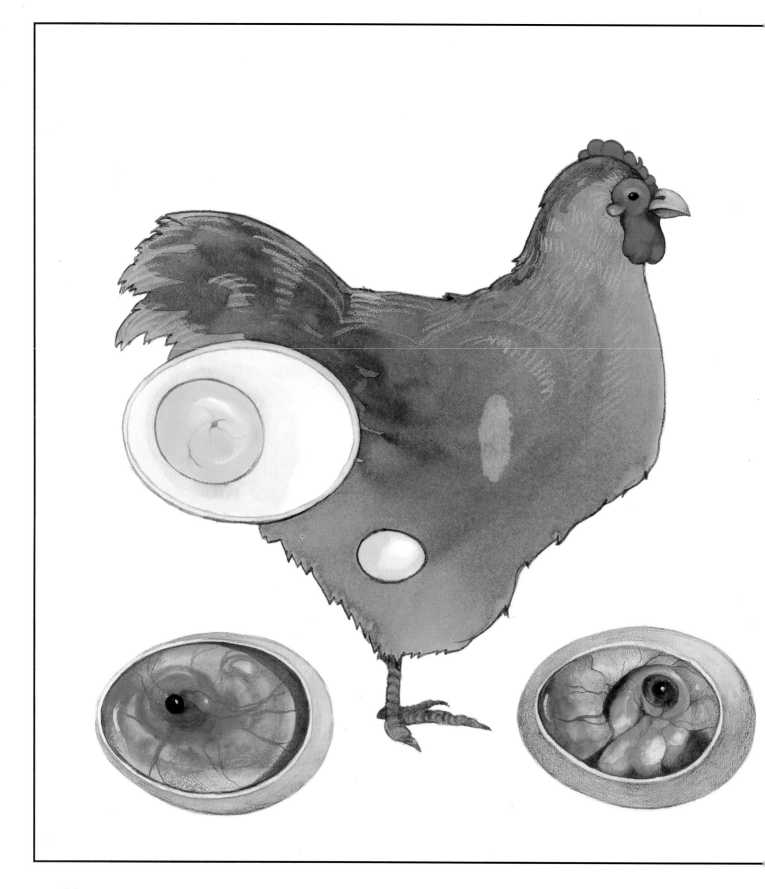

How does an **EGG** become a chicken?

A chicken egg is made inside the body of the female chicken, the hen.

There are three parts of an egg: the *yolk,* the *white,* and the *shell.* The growing baby chick gets its food from the yolk and is protected by the white and the shell. While the chick grows, it must be kept warm.

It takes 21 days for the chick to grow big enough to hatch. By the third day, its brain, ears, and eyes are forming. By the fifth day, its wings and legs have begun to grow. By the seventeenth day, the chick has fine little feathers. Finally, after three weeks, the chick is born. It has gotten too big for the shell and breaks out or hatches.

What is **FIRE**?

Fire is what we see and feel when something burns. We see fire because it gives off an orange or yellow glow, called a *flame*. We feel fire because it gives off *heat*.

In ancient times, people made fire by striking a piece of stone, called *flint,* against another stone. The striking created enough heat to make a spark — a very tiny flame — which could be used to light dry leaves and twigs. These could then be fanned into a larger fire.

Long ago, people used wood as *fuel* for fires. Later, they discovered other things that would burn, like coal or oil. Gas and oil stoves and furnaces use fire to create the heat to cook our food and warm our homes.

Nowadays, we don't use flints to start fires. We use matches. Matches use the same idea. One scratchy surface rubs against another until a spark starts a fire. Remember: Never play with matches, because fire can hurt you!

How do **FISH** breathe?

Take a deep breath . . . and let it out. You are breathing — taking air into your lungs. Air has a gas called *oxygen* mixed in it. All living creatures need oxygen to live. But if you have ever been swimming, you know that you can't breathe in when you put your head underwater. You'll either swallow water or get it up your nose!

A fish has special filters called *gills* on each side of its head. These gills work something like our lungs. A fish takes in water through its mouth, and the gills take oxygen out of the water. The water then passes out of the gills through openings.

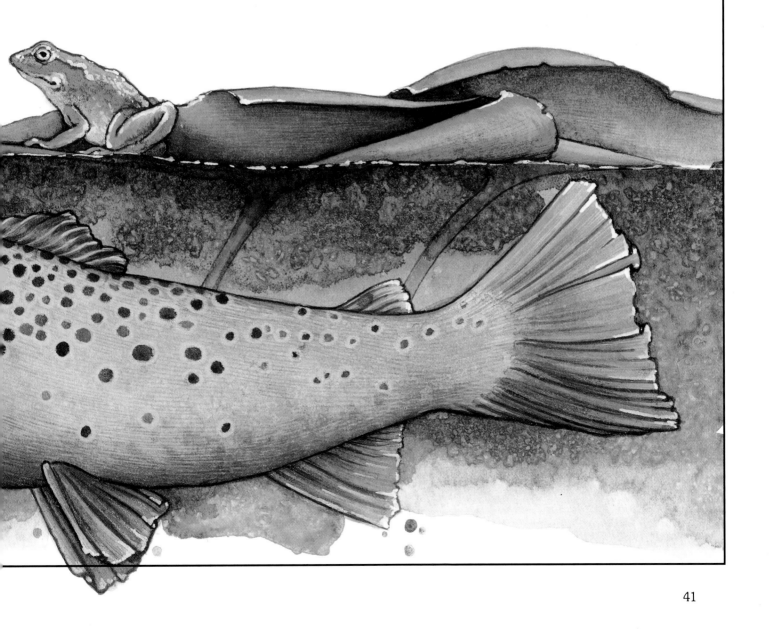

What is a **FLAG**?

A flag is a piece of cloth that has a special design and special colors. A flag is a *symbol.* A symbol stands for, or makes us think about, something else. A heart on a Valentine's Day card is a symbol for love.

Long ago, families and tribes had their own flags. Now, countries and states have flags. If you wave the flag of your country, it's a way of showing that your country is important to you. American astronauts left their flag on the moon so everyone who visits the moon will know someone from the United States has already been there.

What are **FRECKLES**?

Freckles are spots on your skin made by a chemical in your body called *melanin*. Melanin is a *pigment*. Pigments give color to parts of an animal or plant. Melanin is a pigment that is dark brown or black. Almost everyone has some melanin in his or her skin.

If there is a lot of melanin in one place on the skin, a dark spot appears. We call that a freckle. Lots of people have freckles. You might have some yourself.

You are more likely to have freckles if your parents or grandparents do — just as you may have the same color hair as your mom or be tall like your grandfather.

Where does **GARBAGE** go?

In most places, garbage is picked up by a truck. Then, several different things can happen. The garbage might be taken to a dump or *landfill*. It might be taken to an *incinerator,* a huge oven that burns garbage. Or it might be put on a flat boat called a *barge* and dropped in the ocean.

Because dumps and landfills are filling up everywhere, we have to cut down on the garbage we throw away. Some garbage — like tin cans, glass bottles, or newspapers — can be *recycled*. That means that they can be used again.

Many people save leftover foods, grass cuttings, and leaves to make *compost*. Compost contains vitamins and minerals. When compost is put back in the earth, it makes the soil richer.

Why do people wear **GLASSES**?

Some people need help to see things clearly because their eyes don't work as well as they should. If people are *nearsighted,* they wear glasses to help them see faraway objects better. If they are *farsighted,* their glasses help them see objects that are close by. Everybody's eyes are different, so each pair of glasses is specially made to work for the person who wears them.

You've probably seen lots of people wearing glasses. Maybe you even wear them yourself. More than 100 million people in the United States do!

Glasses can also help eyes grow stronger. Some people have weak muscles in one eye that keep it from looking in the right direction. Glasses train the muscles to work the way they should.

Some people wear *contact lenses* instead of glasses. These are very small, and fit right into the eye so that they don't show at all.

Why does **GRAVITY** make things fall down?

If an apple drops from a tree, it falls down. It stops when it reaches the ground. But if it kept on going, it would head toward the center of the earth. The center of the earth is always pulling on everything that is on its surface.

We call the force of earth's pulling an object, like an apple, *gravity*. If earth didn't have gravity, guess where you'd be right now? Somewhere off in space! Without earth's gravity, there would be nothing to hold you down to the planet.

The moon has less gravity than the earth. So the moon doesn't pull on you as hard. That's why, when the astronauts visited the moon, they just bounced around.

What makes **HAIR** grow?

Each hair on your head starts to grow from a root underneath the scalp. At the end of the root is a soft structure called the *hair bulb*. Cells in the hair bulb divide quickly. As the new cells form, they push the older cells upward and through the skin.

The root is the only part of a hair that is alive. That's why it doesn't hurt to cut the ends of your hair. A healthy head may have as many as one hundred thousand strands of hair. Even though you can lose fifty or one hundred hairs every day, your body is always busy growing more.

What is a **HOLIDAY**?

A holiday is a day set aside for celebrating a special event or remembering something important that happened a long time ago. Life would be pretty boring if everyone had to go to work or school all the time and if every day were the same. It's nice to have holidays to look forward to. They help make the year fun and interesting!

On many holidays, people eat certain foods, enjoy each other's company, and think about what makes the day special.

On a national holiday like the Fourth of July, people celebrate the birthday of the United States. On religious holidays, like Christmas and Passover, people gather to worship God.

Every country has its own holidays. Some countries have holidays just for children. In China, there is a boys' holiday called Kite-Flying Day. And in Japan, there is a girls' holiday called Doll Day.

Independence Day (Fourth of July)

Christmas

Thanksgiving

Chinese New Year

Ii

What is **ICE**?

There are three kinds of matter in the world: *liquids* (such as water, milk, and lemonade); *solids* (things like rocks, chairs, and dogs); and *gases* (such as air, and the helium in helium balloons). But sometimes one kind of matter can change into another.

When the temperature of the air reaches 32 degrees on a Fahrenheit thermometer, water freezes. The water changes from a liquid to a solid — ice. That's why, when it turns cold in the winter, the surfaces of ponds and lakes freeze. Then you can go ice skating on the top of the pond while the fish are swimming below.

What is **ICE CREAM**?

Ice cream is a frozen *custard* made from milk, cream, sugar, and flavorings. Is there anyone who doesn't like ice cream? Summer or winter, it's a wonderful treat!

The milk and other ingredients are mixed and poured into a *churn*. A churn is a special freezer that looks like a deep, covered bowl. Everything is stirred until it freezes. The stirring keeps the mixture from getting too hard and icy.

Some churns can make ice cream for hundreds of people. But there are also churns that are the right size for families to use at home. There are even kid-size churns that make just enough ice cream to fill one cone!

People have been enjoying ice cream for thousands of years. In ancient Rome, people sometimes ate ice cream made out of snow brought down from the mountains!

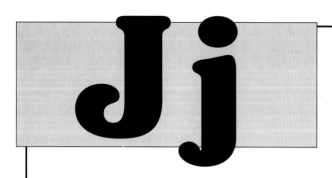

Jj

What is a **JUNGLE**?

A jungle is a very thick forest that is always warm and wet. The weather is perfect for plants to grow so there are many different kinds of trees and bushes and vines. There are jungles in many parts of Africa, Asia, and South America.

Many animals live in the jungle. The hippopotamus lives in the jungles of Africa. Monkeys and parrots live in the South American jungles. Tigers are found only in the Asian jungles, but there are snakes in all of them. People live in jungles, too. They may hunt animals, gather fruits, berries, nuts, and other foods, or even farm the land.

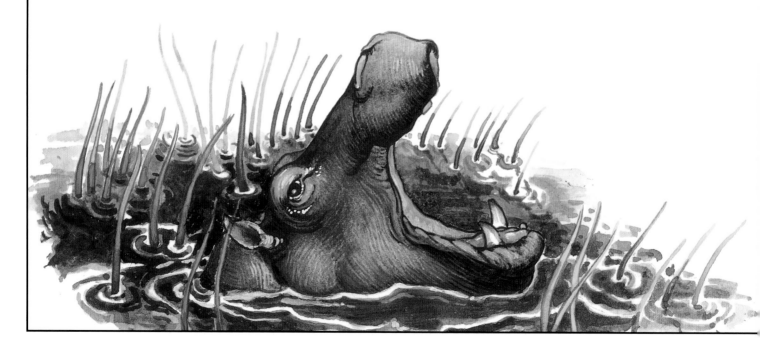

What makes a **KITE** fly?

Wind makes a kite fly.

A kite, whether it is made of paper or cloth, works the same way as an airplane, only without an engine. When you fly a kite, you run against the wind, pulling the kite behind you with a string.

The wind is *pushing* hard against the kite, while you are *pulling* in the other direction. In order to get away from your pulling and the wind's pushing, the kite is usually forced up. Sometimes the kite goes down instead, and you have to try again.

Just make sure your string is very strong!

L1

What makes **LEAVES** change color?

Leaves get their color from *pigments*. The pigment called *chlorophyll* makes a leaf green. There are other pigments for red and yellow inside the leaves, too. During the spring and summer, when the sun is strong, leaves have more chlorophyll.

When autumn comes, there is less sun. Soon the chlorophyll, and therefore the green color inside the leaf, disappears. Now the other colors, such as yellow and red and orange, can appear.

filament

What's inside a **LIGHT BULB**?

Inside a light bulb there is a very thin wire, called a *filament*. The filament is connected in two places to a metal plate at the bottom of the bulb. When a lamp is turned on, electricity flows through the plate, and up through the filament inside the light bulb.

The electricity makes the filament very hot — white hot — almost burning. The hot filament gives off a bright white glow. The shape of the bulb makes the light shine brightly in all directions.

What is **MONEY**?

Money is what you use to buy things you need or want. If you need a pair of sneakers from a store, then you have to give the store owner something in exchange for the sneakers. With money, we trade for things like food and toys or even cars and houses.

Most grown-ups earn their money by going to work. A person may be paid a certain amount of money for each hour or year he or she works. Have you ever helped with chores at home and been paid for it?

You may have a piggy bank at home that holds coins like pennies, nickels, dimes, and quarters. This is a good place to save your money. And when it is full, you'll be able to buy something you really want!

What is the **MOON**?

The moon is a gray, rocky ball — a huge boulder in space. When there is a full moon, it may look like a dim sun. But the light we see is sunlight bouncing off the surface of the moon.

The moon is much smaller than the earth. It has high mountains — some as high as those on earth. The moon also has large, wide holes, called *craters*. Scientists believe craters were made by large rocks called *meteorites* that crashed into the moon's surface from space. The craters and mountains create shadows on the surface, and those shadows sometimes look to us like a face that we call the "Man in the Moon."

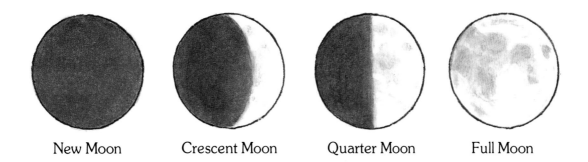

New Moon   Crescent Moon   Quarter Moon   Full Moon

What is the **NORTH POLE**?

The earth is a gigantic ball that is slightly flat at the top and bottom. It *rotates,* or spins, in space like a top. Scientists draw an imaginary line, called the *axis,* from the top of the earth all the way through the center, to the bottom. The end of the axis at the top of the ball is called the North Pole. The one at the bottom is the South Pole.

From anywhere you stand on the earth, if you look north you are looking toward the North Pole; if you look south, you are looking toward the South Pole.

The North and South poles are the coldest places on earth. That is because they never get as much direct sunlight as the rest of the earth. The South Pole is on a continent called Antarctica. Snow and ice cover this continent in most places. The North Pole is actually over water but, since it is always so cold there, the water is covered by a thick layer of ice.

What is the highest **NUMBER**?

What is the highest number you can count to? Is it 100? Of course not! If you can count to 100, then you can count to 101! There is no highest number!

For every number you can think of, there is always a number that is higher. You could spend all week counting and you would never reach the highest number.

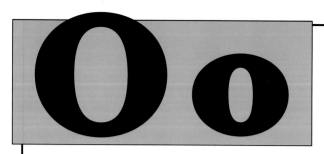

What's at the bottom of the **OCEAN**?

What's at the bottom of your room? A floor. The ocean has a floor, too. Just like the ground on land, the ocean floor has mountains and valleys.

Tiny pieces of rocks, shells, fish bones, and other things that drift down through the ocean water collect on the bottom and cover the ocean floor. This is called *sediment*.

Fish swim just above the ocean floor. Sometimes there are plants on the bottom, but only if it is close enough to the ocean's surface. Only there can the plants get the sunlight they need to grow.

Over the years, many ships have sunk to the bottom of the ocean — sometimes from bad storms, or from damage through a battle at sea. Some of these ships carried treasure and many of them are still on the bottom of the ocean, just waiting for someone to find them!

Why do people get **OLD**?

No one really knows exactly why we get old. We do know that our bodies change over the years. You probably have noticed that your own body is getting bigger all the time.

As people get older, though, their bodies start acting differently. Young bodies work on growing bones and muscles and teeth. Older bodies slow down this building process and change in other ways, too.

Most people agree that "oldness" doesn't just depend on how many years you've lived. Everyone gets old — or ages — differently. A lot depends on how well you take care of yourself. If you eat healthy foods and exercise regularly, you will probably live longer. And, if your parents and other people in your family live a long time, chances are that you will, too.

Pp

Where does **PAPER** come from?

Paper is made by taking tiny threads called *fibers* from a plant or tree and pressing them on a screen under water that runs very fast. The fibers are pressed together and dried to form a flat, thin sheet.

The paper we use today mostly comes from chopped-up trees and is made by large machines. Because trees take a long time to grow, we should be careful to *recycle* paper so that it can be used again.

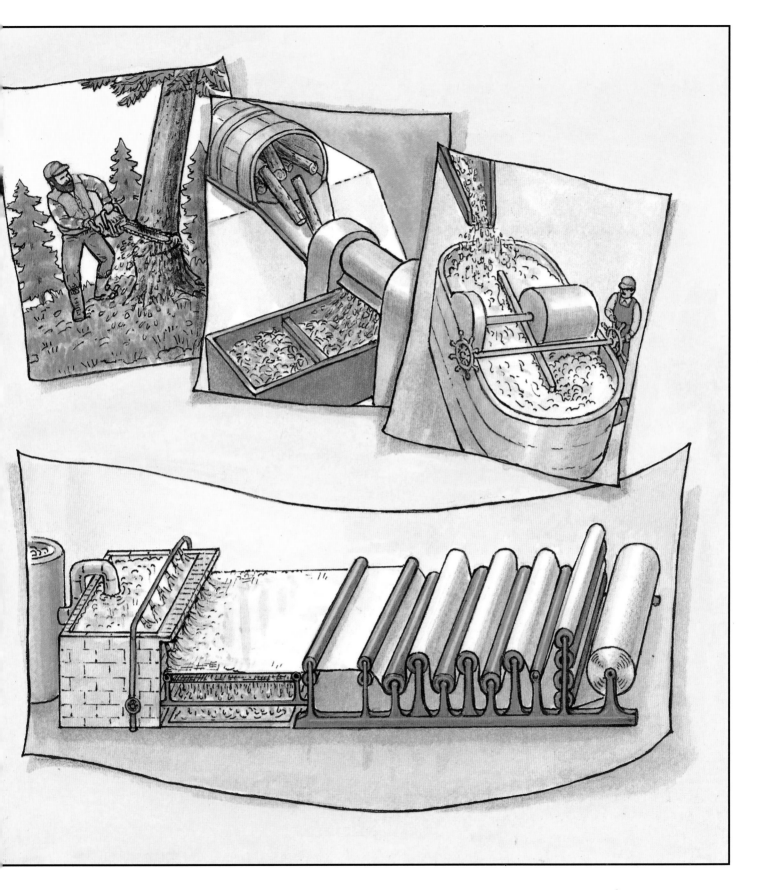

Why are **PEOPLE** different colors?

All over the world, people are different colors. That is because they, or their parents, come from many parts of the world. People who come from warm countries, like those in Africa, usually have darker skin than those who come from colder countries, like those in northern Europe.

Your body has a chemical called *melanin*. Melanin is a *pigment,* and pigments give color to your skin. Melanin is the pigment that controls shades of brown. It reacts to the sun. That is why people whose ancestors lived in hot countries have darker skin. And the shades vary depending on where your family originally came from.

People may be different colors, but all people — no matter what color — eat, sleep, laugh, cry, work, play, and dream.

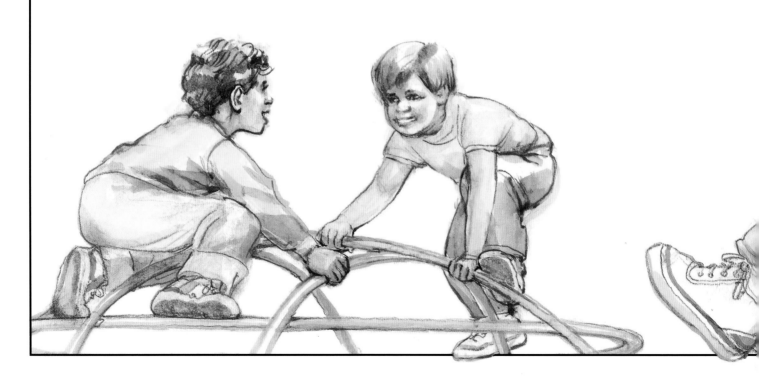

What is a **QUEEN**?

A queen is a woman who is either the leader of a country or who is married to the leader, the *king*. England, Holland, and Spain are some countries that have queens and kings.

In the United States there are no queens or kings. American citizens hold elections every four years to vote on who will be the leader of the country. The winner of the vote is called the *president*.

The president can only be president for eight years. But once a girl or woman becomes a queen, she will be one for the rest of her life. In England, Victoria was the queen for over 60 years — from 1837 to 1901!

What makes a **RAINBOW**?

A rainbow is made when sunlight shines through raindrops in the air. Sometimes after a summer shower, the sun comes out again and shines through a part of the sky where there are still some raindrops.

Light from the sun or a light bulb may look white, but it's really a mixture of many colors. Usually, we can't see these colors. But sometimes these colors become visible. If the sunlight hits the raindrops at a certain angle, the colors in the white light break apart. This brings the different colors out of the white light. These colors then form a beautiful rainbow, an arc of colors across the sky.

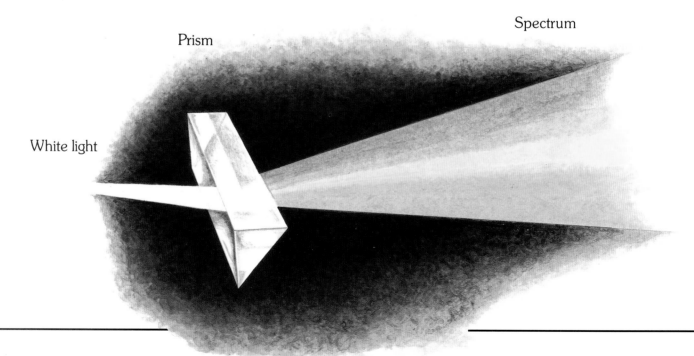

Prism

Spectrum

White light

How does a **ROCKET** get to outer space?

A rocket uses *fuel* to make power for the engine. The fuel is set on fire inside the rocket. As the fuel burns, it creates gases that have great pressure. These gases are blasted out of the rocket engines.

These gases all go out the bottom of the rocket where it is open. They come out so fast and with so much power that the rocket is pushed up. It is pushed up so hard that the rocket overcomes the force of gravity, which tries to keep everything on the ground. The force that pushes up against the front of the rocket is called *thrust*.

Unlike an airplane, a rocket does not use wings to help it fly. It just uses the power and force created by the burning fuel to make enough thrust.

S s

Why do the **SEASONS** change?

The seasons change because the earth is always traveling around the sun. The sun provides light and heat on earth. It takes 365 days, or one year, for the earth to make one complete circle, or *orbit,* around the sun.

As it travels around the sun, the earth is tilted, or turned slightly to one side. Because of this, some places on the earth are tilted toward the sun and receive more of its heat and light. Other places on earth, which are tilted away, receive less.

When a place is tilted away from the sun, it is winter there and the days are cold and short. When a place is tilted toward the sun, it is summer there and the days are warm and long.

WINTER

SPRING

FALL

SUMMER

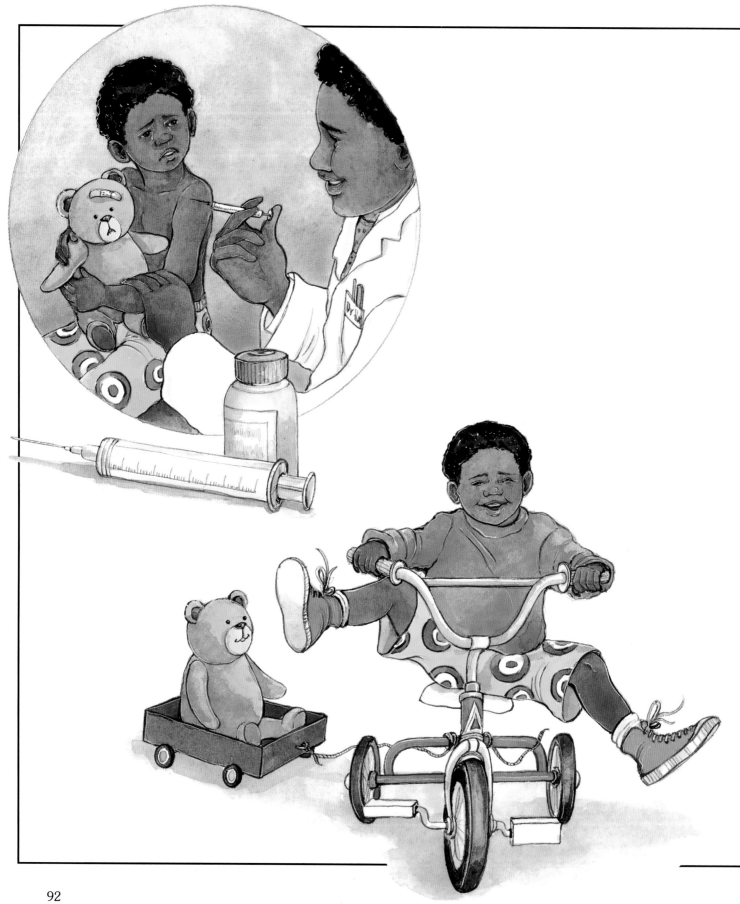

Why do doctors give **SHOTS**?

If you get sick, you may need medicine. Usually, a medicine has to travel all through your body to work. If you swallow a spoonful of medicine, it travels first to your stomach, and from there into your blood stream. The blood then carries the medicine to the part of your body that needs it.

But some medicines won't work quickly enough if they are swallowed. Then the doctor may give you a shot so that the medicine can help you get better faster.

Sometimes the doctor will give you a shot even when you're not sick! That may not seem fair, but some shots contain medicines that will keep you from getting sick later. So they really are good for you.

You might think getting a shot hurts, but it's only for a short while. And think how bad it feels to be sick!

Why do I have to **SLEEP**?

At the end of the day, your body and brain are tired, even if you don't realize it. Sleep brings back the energy you'll need for the next day.

Do you like to go to sleep at night? Lots of kids don't. Neither do some grown-ups! But everyone needs to sleep. Sleeping is one of the most important ways our bodies keep healthy.

While you sleep, your body works extra hard to grow and stay strong. If you get sick, extra sleep will help you get better fast. Even dreaming is good for you.

When people don't get enough sleep, it's hard for them to pay attention. They may have trouble learning new things. Sometimes, when people haven't slept for a really long time, they might even have trouble seeing and hearing. But once they catch up on their sleep, they are fine.

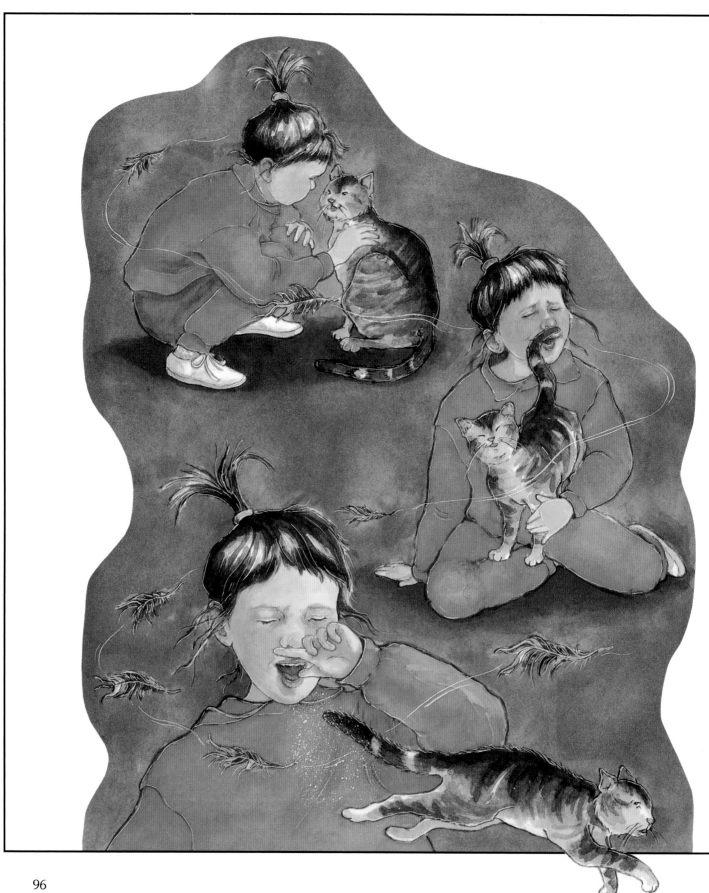

What makes me **SNEEZE**?

A sneeze is caused by a tickle! It's like a tickle on your foot or tummy, but way back behind your nose. Something tiny — like a piece of dust — gets in there.

    You know how you scrunch up your foot when someone tickles it? When something tickles the inside of your nose, your chest and stomach scrunch up by themselves.

    As your muscles tighten, you take a long, deep breath. You fill up with air. Finally, when you feel you're about to burst, your muscles suddenly unscrunch and you let out a tremendous sneeze. Whatever was tickling you is gone!

What makes the **STARS** shine?

The stars we see in the night sky are gigantic balls of very hot gases. The gases are so hot, they give off light.

Because stars are so very far away in space, they look to us like tiny, twinkling dots.

Our sun is a star that is much closer to the earth than any other star. During the day, our sun is so bright that we can't see the other stars shine. But they are there all the time just the same.

Tt

What are **TEETH** made of?

Teeth are the hardest things in our bodies — even harder than bones. The part of the tooth we can see is called the *crown.* It is covered with *enamel,* a very hard layer that protects the tooth.

Babies are born without teeth. Most babies are about six to nine months old when their first teeth grow in. The growing-in time is called teething, and the new teeth are called baby teeth. Sometimes teething hurts a little, and babies may be cranky.

As children grow, their mouths grow too, so they need a new set of larger teeth. From the ages of six or seven to twelve years or so, your 20 baby teeth will fall out one by one. They are pushed out by 32 new teeth called permanent teeth. With good care, permanent teeth will never fall out.

The enamel on your teeth is very, very strong, but to stay strong it must be kept clean. So be sure to brush your teeth after every meal and visit your dentist for regular check-ups.

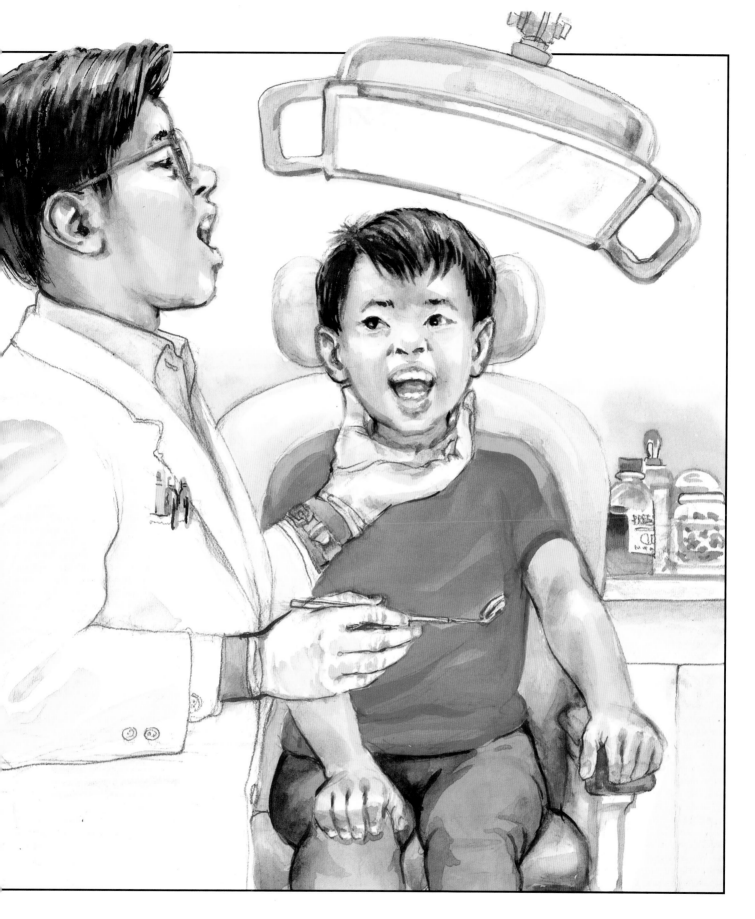

What is a **TORNADO**?

A tornado is a very strong windstorm shaped like a *funnel*. It can knock down houses, trees, and almost anything else in its path.

Like thunderstorms, tornadoes form in the clouds. When warm, wet air meets cooler air, sometimes a swirling motion starts up inside the clouds. This funnel of wind dips down from the clouds and sometimes touches the ground. A tornado moves very fast.

If a tornado hits the ground, it acts like a gigantic vacuum cleaner. It can suck up dirt, rocks, or even cars and set them down miles away!

What makes a **TREE** grow?

A tree starts out as a tiny *seed,* which contains everything it needs to grow. Trees have *roots* that push down into the dirt. As the tree gets older and bigger, the roots beneath the ground grow too, although you can't see them. Trees use their roots to drink up water and get food and vitamins from the soil.

Every year the tree lives, it forms another layer of tissue called *cambium.* Cambium is like a thick version of our own skin. After a tree is cut down, you can tell its age by counting these layers, or *annual rings,* in the trunk. There is one ring for each year of a tree's life.

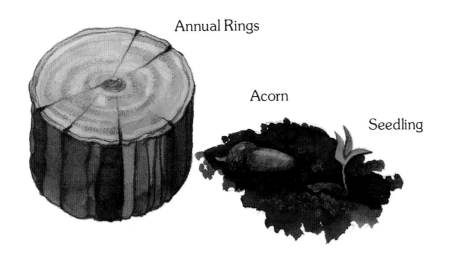

Annual Rings

Acorn

Seedling

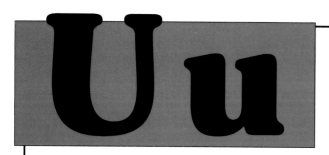

What is a **UFO**?

The letters UFO stand for the words *Unidentified Flying Object*. If something is called a UFO it means that it has been seen flying in the air, but that no one knows exactly what it is or where it came from. Some people think UFOs are visitors from another planet, travelling in spaceships called flying saucers.

Many people say they have seen UFOs, but it usually turns out that they saw something quite ordinary. A plane, car headlights, or even a kite can look strange sometimes, especially at night. What if you saw a plane that was so far away it looked like blinking lights? You might not realize it was a plane — you might think it was a UFO!

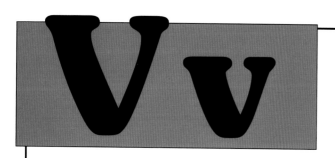

What is a **VOLCANO**?

A volcano is a crack in the earth that goes from its surface down to the hot, melted rocks far below. These rocks are called *magma*. When the boiling magma is forced up through the crack to the earth's surface, it loses its gases and becomes lava. Then we say the volcano has *erupted.*

A volcano erupts because of pressure in the gases that are trapped inside the magma. Some volcanoes erupt very violently; others are milder. Scientists can sometimes tell when a volcano will erupt by measuring movements in the earth nearby.

Many volcanoes look like mountains. These mountains are formed by many layers of lava. After each eruption, the lava eventually cools and forms rock. The Hawaiian islands are made of layers of lava from volcanoes.

Earth isn't the only planet with volcanoes — some other planets have them, too!

Ww

What is a **WEDDING**?

A wedding is a *ceremony* that takes place when a man and a woman decide that they want to spend their lives together. The man is called the *groom* and the woman is called the *bride*.

Some weddings are small and simple, and only a few close family members or friends are there.

At a big fancy wedding, the bride and groom have helpers called attendants. The groom has ushers and a best man, often his brother or best friend. The bride has bridesmaids and a maid or matron of honor. You may have been a flower girl or a ring bearer in someone's wedding.

Weddings can take place in a house of worship, like a church or synagogue, or in a home or garden. Usually, a priest, rabbi, or justice of the peace performs the ceremony and makes the marriage official.

What makes the **WIND** blow?

Wind is air that moves. Instead of saying the air is moving, we say the wind is blowing.

Air is made up of tiny particles called *molecules*. When the air is heated by the sun, its molecules move faster and spread out. As they do, the air gets lighter and it rises.

As the heated air rises, cooler, heavier air moves in to take its place. Because cooler air takes the place of heated air, we usually find wind to be cooling. But sometimes on very hot days there is no wind, only a warm breeze.

Because the sun does not heat different parts of the earth evenly, it can be windy in one place, but not in another.

Why do people **WORK**?

Most people work to earn money to buy the things they need for themselves and their families. Some people work at caring for their children because children need adults to teach them. Others work because it feels good to get a job done. Children work, too. Learning is the work they do. Even animals have to work to find food and build homes. Everyone works — and that's how the world works!

Can you imagine what the world would be like if nobody worked? There would be no doctors to cure us when we got sick or farmers to grow our food. There would be no one to take care of children and no teachers to teach them. There would be no books, because no one would write them. There would be no cities or towns. There would be no stores or clothes or toys. Houses, roads, and cars could never be built. The world would be a very dreary place.

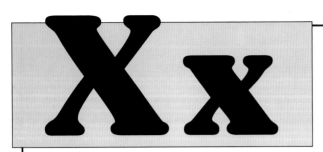

What is an **X Ray**?

An X-ray camera takes a special kind of picture of the inside of your body. The camera sends out special light rays that you can't see. These light rays pass through your soft tissues (the skin and muscles) but not through hard tissues like your bones and teeth.

If you have a bad fall and your arm hurts, the doctor will probably take an X ray to see if any bones are broken. Dentists use them, too, to check your teeth for cavities.

X rays don't hurt. But you have to sit very still when the picture is taken. Otherwise it might look like you have blurry arm bones!

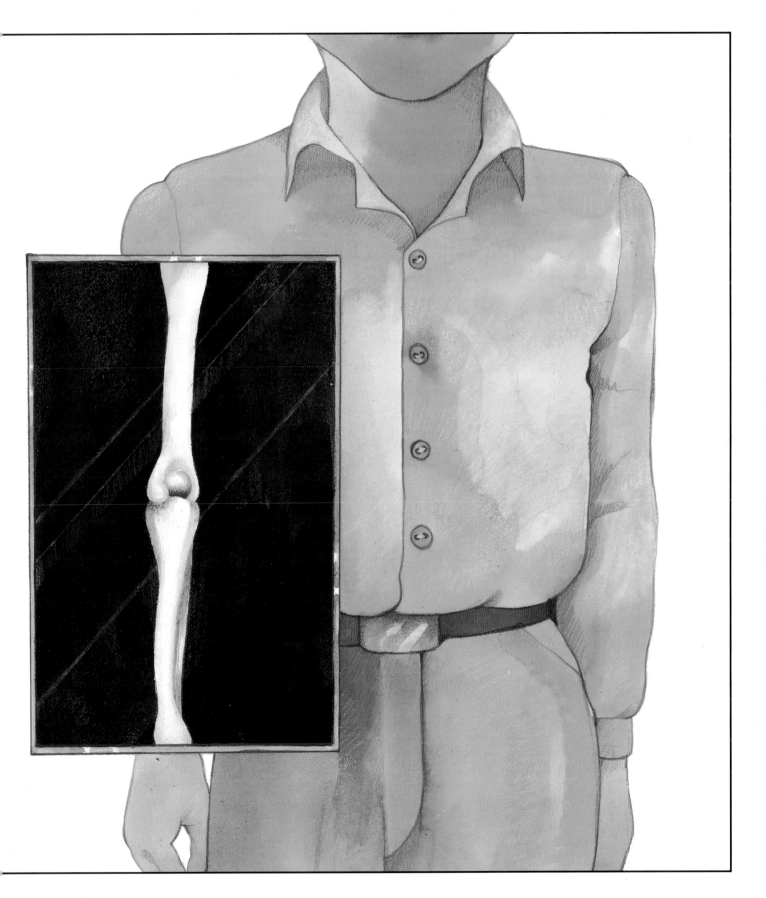

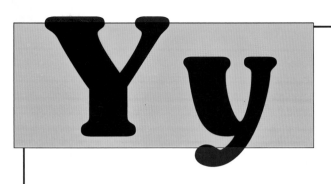

Why do people **YAWN**?

Did you know that mice yawn? It's true. So do dogs, cats — and people. The funny thing is that no one knows exactly *why* we yawn!

Of course, everyone knows *when* we yawn. People and animals yawn when they are sleepy or bored. One idea about yawning is that it helps people to wake up. Yawns stretch the muscles in the face and neck and help our blood to circulate. That can make us feel more wide-awake.

Scientists also think that people may yawn when they need more oxygen. Getting fresh air or exercise helps give our bodies the oxygen we need. So yawning might be a signal that it's time to start moving.

Here's a funny thing about yawning: it's catching. If you yawn or even just talk about yawning, the people around you will probably start yawning, too. Try it and see!

What makes a **YO-YO** come back up?

When you unwind the string from a yo-yo by letting go of it, you are putting your energy into the yo-yo. The energy is kept there, or stored.

When the yo-yo reaches the bottom of the string, this energy still exists. The yo-yo is still spinning. The energy has to go somewhere. So it is forced to work its way back up the string.

Eventually, a yo-yo will use up all the energy that you put into it when you first set it in motion. Then it will stop spinning.

Zz

Why do **ZEBRAS** have stripes?

The zebra, with its bright black and white stripes, is easy for us to see. But in the grasslands, where the zebra lives, those same stripes help to hide it from lions and other enemies. It is hard for the zebra's enemies to see the stripes against the tall, wavy grasses.

The zebra's stripes help to confuse the lion. When a great many zebras run away, they become a blur of stripes. It's harder for a lion to spot a single zebra.

What is a **ZOO**?

A zoo is a big park filled with wild animals from all over the world. Some of these animals were caught in the wild and brought to the zoo. Some of the animals were born right at the zoo. Sometimes the animals are kept in cages and other times they are allowed to roam free behind fences. Both children and adults like to look at animals.

Have you ever seen a lion from Africa? How about a penguin from Antarctica? Or a Gila monster from the southwestern United States? Even if you don't live near any of these places, you can see these animals at a zoo.

Most zoos try to give their animals comfortable and interesting homes. They want the animals to be as happy as if they were still in the wild.

Many people are needed to take care of the animals in zoos. There are zookeepers, zoo doctors, and even zoo cooks who make meals from meat, fruit, fish, seeds, bugs, and earthworms for the different animals!

Index